THE
"Don't Be Difficult"
WORKBOOK

by Lawrence E. Shapiro, Ph.D.
and Hennie M. Shore

The Center for Applied Psychology, Inc.
King of Prussia, Pennsylvania

The "Don't Be Difficult" Workbook
by Lawrence E. Shapiro, Ph.D. and Hennie M. Shore

Published by: The Center for Applied Psychology, Inc., P.O. Box 61587, King of Prussia, PA 19406 USA Tel. 1.800.962.1141

The Center for Applied Psychology, Inc. is the publisher of Childswork/Childsplay, a catalog of products for mental health professionals, teachers, and parents who wish to help children with their social and emotional growth.

ISBN: 1-882732-64-2

Introduction for Adults

There is almost nothing that makes teachers and counselors more frustrated than "difficult" children. These children are oppositional, uncooperative, and even defiant. Adults want to help them, but, by definition, these children don't want to be helped. Difficult children constantly test the rules and thwart our best efforts.

Many professionals recommend using behavior modification techniques to help difficult children, rewarding appropriate behaviors and punishing ones that are inappropriate; but while these techniques are helpful, they are often not enough.

This workbook is designed to teach children a cognitive approach to their problems; new ways to think as well as new ways to act. Each exercise in this workbook asks children to consider that there are two ways to approach any problem: one that makes the problem even more serious and one that is more realistic and appropriate. Children are taught that thinking about problems realistically makes it more likely that they will come up with reasonable and helpful solutions.

As children read and respond to the six stories in this workbook, they learn the principles of positive self-talk and how to consider the consequences of their behaviors. They also learn to recognize important values and principles that can guide their behavior.

This book is intended to be used by counselors, teachers, or parents to help children develop more positive ways to deal with their problems. Individual activities can be photocopied from the book and given to children, or the activities can be used as part of a group discussion. Adults working with "difficult" children should remember that these behaviors generally do not change easily or quickly, but a combination of patience, structure, and realistic expectations will eventually make a difference. Good luck!

– The Authors

Introduction For Kids

Some people think that it is easy being a kid, but you and I know differently. There is schoolwork and chores, as well as brothers and sisters who can be a nuisance, and there are always a lot of grown-ups telling you what to do. Being a kid is fun, but it can be hard work too.

Some children seem to make things even harder for themselves. They don't like to obey the rules in their home, and they don't like to cooperate in school. Adults call these children "difficult."

This book was written to help children find better ways to deal with their problems. The message of this book is that: "All children have problems, but you don't have to make things worse for yourself."

The children in the stories in this book have a variety of problems, but certain things that they say or do will make these problems easier and other things will make them harder. Your job is to think of the things that will make things easier for the children in each story.

Hopefully in thinking about how these children can look at their problems a little differently, you can decide if there are things in your own life that you need to change. You can learn to be more positive, to make better choices, and to look for solutions that will really work. Good luck!

– The Authors

Trisha's parents were at the end of their rope. They didn't know what to do about Trisha's horrible disposition. She never cooperated with them and was always causing trouble at home and school.

Trisha was never concerned about doing well in school. One night she stayed up late watching a movie. She didn't study for the math test because she had gotten the answers from a kid who had already taken the test. "This is easy," she thought as she copied the answers from a hidden paper. All of a sudden, a shadow fell on her desk and she looked up to see the teacher standing over her.

On the opposite page, write something that Trisha should say to the teacher. Then write the wrong thing that Trisha could say.

What do you think would happen if Trisha chose the wrong thing to say to the teacher?

_____

_____

_____

What do you think would happen if Trisha chose the right thing to say?

_____

_____

_____

Write a rule or principle that could help Trisha avoid this problem in the future.

_____

_____

_____

Write about a situation in which you got in trouble for breaking the rules. What happened? What do you think is the best way to avoid making things worse in this kind of situation?

_____

_____

_____

4

As if the test episode wasn't enough for Trisha, she had to make more trouble for herself.

"You're so fat that I thought a bus was coming at me down the hall!" Trisha yelled to Owen as he passed. "Do you have a problem with me?" Owen asked her. "Let's talk about it," he challenged.

On the opposite page, write something that Trisha should say to Owen. Then write the wrong thing that Trisha could say.

What do you think would happen if Trisha chose the wrong thing to say to Owen?

_____

_____

_____

What do you think would happen if Trisha chose the right thing to say?

_____

_____

_____

Write a rule or principle that could help Trisha avoid this problem in the future.

_____

_____

_____

Write about a situation in which you were mean to someone for no real reason (or someone was mean to you). What happened? What do you think is the best way to avoid making things worse in this kind of situation?

_____

_____

_____

THE
WRONG THING
TO SAY

_____
_____
_____
_____
_____

THE
RIGHT THING
TO SAY

_____
_____
_____
_____

7

As bad as Trisha's attitude was, some people still wanted to give her a chance. After seeing Trisha get into trouble with the teacher, a group of kids asked Trisha if she wanted to study for the history test with them. "They must think I'm stupid," she thought. "I don't need anybody's help."

On the opposite page, write something that Trisha should say to the group. Then write the wrong thing that Trisha could say.

What do you think would happen if Trisha chose the wrong thing to say to the group?

_____

_____

_____

What do you think would happen if Trisha chose the right thing to say?

_____

_____

_____

Write a rule or principle that could help Trisha avoid this problem in the future.

_____

_____

_____

Write about a situation in which you thought someone was teasing or mocking you. What happened? What do you think is the best way to avoid making things worse in this kind of situation?

_____

_____

_____

8

THE WRONG THING TO SAY

THE RIGHT THING TO SAY

9

Finally, Trisha's grades were so terrible that she decided not to go to school anymore. After her parents left for work, she just stayed home. A few days later, the teacher called. "Why haven't you been at school?" her dad asked her.

On the opposite page, write something that Trisha should say to her dad. Then write the wrong thing that Trisha could say.

What do you think would happen if Trisha chose the wrong thing to say to her dad?

_____

_____

_____

What do you think would happen if Trisha chose the right thing to say?

_____

_____

_____

Write a rule or principle that could help Trisha avoid this problem in the future.

_____

_____

_____

Write about a situation which you felt was so hopeless that you almost gave up. What happened? What do you think is the best way to avoid making things worse in this kind of situation?

_____

_____

_____

Now Trisha's troubles were really starting to pile up. It was bad enough that she alienated everyone at school, but now she was starting to do the same thing with the kids in her neighborhood.

Lonnie told Trisha he wanted to use her roller blades. "Too bad," said Trisha. "I don't lend my things." "But when I let you use my bike, you said I could use your blades," complained Lonnie. "I changed my mind," Trisha said, walking away.

On the opposite page, write something that Trisha should say to Lonnie. Then write the wrong thing that Trisha could say.

What do you think would happen if Trisha chose the wrong thing to say to Lonnie?

_____

_____

_____

What do you think would happen if Trisha chose the right thing to say?

_____

_____

_____

Write a rule or principle that could help Trisha avoid this problem in the future.

_____

_____

_____

Write about a situation in which you broke a promise or a trust (or someone did this to you). What happened? What do you think is the best way to avoid making things worse in this kind of situation?

_____

_____

_____

When Trisha got home, she was greeted by her mother who informed her that her grandmother broke her hip and had to go to the hospital. The shopping trip for Trisha's birthday present would have to be postponed. Almost immediately Trisha thought, "She did this on purpose so we couldn't go." When she went to visit her grandmother, she was so mad that she could hardly look at her.

On the opposite page, write something that Trisha should say to her grandmother. Then write the wrong thing that Trisha could say.

What do you think would happen if Trisha chose the wrong thing to say to her grandmother?

_____

_____

_____

What do you think would happen if Trisha chose the right thing to say?

_____

_____

_____

Write a rule or principle that could help Trisha avoid this problem in the future.

_____

_____

_____

Write about a situation in which someone disappointed you. What happened? What do you think is the best way to avoid making things worse in this kind of situation?

_____

_____

_____

14

When she arrived back at home, Trisha was so excited when her aunt gave her a birthday present. "I know it's the doll I want," she thought as she opened it. But inside was the wrong doll. "I can't believe it!" she shrieked angrily. "I don't want THIS!"

On the opposite page, write something that Trisha should say to her aunt. Then write the wrong thing that Trisha could say.

What do you think would happen if Trisha chose the wrong thing to say to her aunt?

_____

_____

_____

What do you think would happen if Trisha chose the right thing to say?

_____

_____

_____

Write a rule or principle that could help Trisha avoid this problem in the future.

_____

_____

_____

Write about a situation in which someone gave you something that you really didn't want. How did you handle it? What do you think is the best way to avoid making things worse in this kind of situation?

_____

_____

_____

16

Trisha knew she shouldn't have done it, but she wasn't in the mood to stop and think. In her eyes, her birthday was a disaster, so why not make it worse? She pushed her brother into her birthday cake. "Trisha, you are the one who ruined your birthday!" Trisha's mother shouted at her. "How could you do that?!"

On the opposite page, write something that Trisha should say to her mother and brother. Then write the wrong thing that Trisha could say.

What do you think would happen if Trisha chose the wrong thing to say to her mother and brother?

_____

_____

_____

What do you think would happen if Trisha chose the right thing to say?

_____

_____

_____

Write a rule or principle that could help Trisha avoid this problem in the future.

_____

_____

_____

Write about a situation in which you did something bad without thinking about the consequences first. What happened? What do you think is the best way to avoid making things worse in this kind of situation?

_____

_____

_____

18

19

Trisha spent some time alone thinking about the events that had occurred. She had gone back and forth blaming everyone else for everything that had happened. After a while, she went downstairs and into the living room where her parents were sitting with the rest of the family.

On the opposite page, write something that Trisha should say to her parents. Then write the wrong thing that Trisha could say.

What do you think would happen if Trisha chose the wrong thing to say to her parents?

_____

_____

_____

What do you think would happen if Trisha chose the right thing to say?

_____

_____

_____

Write a rule or principle that could help Trisha avoid this problem in the future.

_____

_____

_____

Write about a situation in which you were expected to do something that you felt was unfair. What happened? What do you think is the best way to avoid making things worse in this kind of situation?

_____

_____

_____

20

21

Everything in Rick's life was so messed up. Even his mom was being mean to him. She had promised him they could go to the mall, but now she said she was too busy. She couldn't take him to a friend's house either, because she had too much to do.

On the opposite page, write the right thing that Rick should say to his mother. Then write the wrong thing that Rick could say to his mother.

What do you think would happen if Rick chose the wrong thing to say to his mother?

_____

_____

_____

What do you think would happen if Rick chose the right thing to say to his mother?

_____

_____

_____

Write a rule or principle that could help Rick deal with similar problems in the future.

_____

_____

_____

Write about a situation in which you were about to lose your temper. Did you lose it? What happened? What do you think is the best way to keep your temper and avoid making things worse?

_____

_____

_____

22

THE
WRONG THING
TO SAY

THE
RIGHT THING
TO SAY

23

Rick was tired of everyone yelling at him. He felt like he couldn't do anything right. When his father told him that he was disappointed that Rick's grades were so bad, Rick felt like he couldn't take it anymore. He felt like he wanted to explode!

On the opposite page, write the right thing that Rick should say to his father. Then write the wrong thing that Rick could say to his father.

What do you think would happen if Rick chose the wrong thing to say to his father?

_____

_____

_____

What do you think would happen if Rick chose the right thing to say to his father?

_____

_____

_____

Write a rule or principle that could help Rick deal with similar problems in the future.

_____

_____

_____

Write about a situation in which you were ready to lose your temper. Did you lose it? What happened? What do you think is the best way to keep your temper and avoid making things worse?

_____

_____

_____

25

When Rick entered his history class, it hit him—he had totally forgotten that there was a test that day! He hadn't even read the chapter, much less studied the information.

On the opposite page, write an excuse that Rick might be thinking that would get him out of the situation (although it wouldn't really help). Then write something that Rick might say to his teacher that would help him now or in the future.

What do you think would happen if Rick chose the wrong thing to do in this situation?

_____

_____

_____

What do you think would happen if Rick chose the right thing?

_____

_____

_____

Write a rule or principle that could help Rick deal with a problem that called for quick action in the future.

_____

_____

_____

Write about a time when you got caught in a similar situation. What would have been the best way to resolve that situation?

_____

_____

_____

On the playground, Rick was being teased by an older group of kids. They said bad things about him, his mother and his younger sister. He felt like fighting, but it would be him against the three bigger kids.

On the opposite page, write the thing that would get Rick into more trouble. Then write the right thing that Rick could say to get himself out of the situation.

What do you think would happen if Rick chose the wrong thing to do in this situation?

_____

_____

_____

What do you think would happen if Rick chose the right thing?

_____

_____

_____

Write a rule or principle that could help Rick deal with similar problems in the future.

_____

_____

_____

Write about a situation in which you were being teased and you really wanted to fight. Did you fight? What do you think is the best way to keep calm and avoid making things worse?

_____

_____

_____

28

THE WRONG THING TO SAY

_____
_____
_____
_____
_____

THE RIGHT THING TO SAY

_____
_____
_____
_____
_____

29

There was nothing that Rick liked more than candy. As far as he was concerned, it was the only food worth eating. He constantly argued with his parents about what he should eat and what he shouldn't eat, and he was often sent to his room because he argued so much at mealtime. Once his father told Rick that if he didn't eat his broccoli, he'd have to sit at the table all night. Rick put all the broccoli in his mouth at one time but couldn't stand the taste. He thought, "Maybe I'll just spit it out—that'll show him."

On the facing page, write another thought Rick might be having that would make the situation worse. Then write something he could be thinking that could make the situation better.

What do you think would happen if Rick chose the wrong thing to do in this situation?

_____

_____

_____

What do you think would happen if Rick chose the right thing?

_____

_____

_____

Write a rule or principle that could help Rick deal with similar problems in the future.

_____

_____

_____

Write about a situation in which you felt that you hated something so much that you would do anything to avoid it. What would have been the best way to resolve that situation?

_____

_____

_____

One Saturday morning, Rick's mother got a call from the manager of the corner drugstore. He told Rick's mother that he had seen Rick taking some candy, and he wanted Rick to bring it back. Rick's mother was very angry when she asked him if he had stolen the candy. Rick had taken three candy bars and hidden them under his bed. But he was afraid to tell his mother what he had done.

On the opposite page, write the wrong thing Rick might say that would make things worse. Then write the right thing for Rick to say to begin to deal with the situation.

What do you think would happen if Rick chose the wrong thing to say to his mother?

_____

_____

_____

What do you think would happen if Rick chose the right thing to say to his mother?

_____

_____

_____

Write a rule or principle that could help Rick deal with a similar problem in the future.

_____

_____

_____

Write about a situation in which you were tempted to take something or in which you actually did take something. What would have been the best way to solve the problem?

_____

_____

_____

33

Rick was always getting into fights with his younger sister. Once he hit her so hard that she fell and sprained her wrist. Rick didn't mean to hurt his little sister, but he couldn't stand her. Rick's father told him to go up to his room and think about how he should punished, and then come down in five minutes and tell him what should be done.

On the opposite page, write something that Rick might feel should be done but would be the wrong thing and make matters worse. Then write something that Rick could say to his father that would help resolve the current situation and make things better between him and his sister in the future.

What do you think would happen if Rick chose the wrong thing to do in this situation?

_____

_____

_____

What do you think would happen if Rick chose the right thing?

_____

_____

_____

Write a rule or principle that could help Rick deal with similar problems in the future.

_____

_____

_____

Write about a situation in which you felt that you hated someone so much that all you wanted to do was bother him or her. What would have been the best way to resolve that situation?

_____

_____

_____

34

THE
WRONG THING
TO SAY

THE
RIGHT THING
TO SAY

35

Sometimes Rick wished all his problems would go away. He imagined that he would find a magic lamp and make three wishes and all the people he didn't like would vanish and only the people he liked would stay.

On the opposite page, write what Rick might be saying to himself (a wish that would not help the problem). Then write something that Rick could wish for that could actually happen and that would help him with his problems.

What do you think would happen if Rick's wrong wish really did come true?

_____

_____

_____

What do you think would happen if the right wish came true?

_____

_____

_____

Write a rule or principle that could help Rick deal with these kinds of feelings in the future.

_____

_____

_____

Write about a time when you felt overwhelmed by your problems. What happened? What would have been the best way to resolve that situation?

_____

_____

_____

Kristen's parents were recently divorced. Things at her house had been really bad for a long time. Now she lived with her mom, and it was a whole lot quieter without her parents fighting all the time. But she still felt angry, and sometimes she felt sad, too.

On one particular afternoon, Kristen took her time walking home from school. She thought about how things used to be before the divorce, and she felt really sad. She decided that when she got home, she'd just go to her room and "chill out." But when she got home, there were some visitors in the living room. Kristen's mom asked her to play the new piano piece she had just learned for the guests. She gave her mom a look that said, "Mom, please don't embarrass me," but her mom kept insisting, saying, "Come on, honey. You're such a good pianist." Finally, she couldn't stand it anymore, and she got ready to say something that would really get her mom to be quiet.

On the opposite page, write the right thing that Kristen should say to her mom. Then write the wrong thing that Kristen could say.

What do you think would happen if Kristen said the wrong thing?

_____

_____

_____

What do you think would happen if Kristen said the right thing?

_____

_____

_____

Write a rule or principle that could help Kristen do the right thing in the future.

_____

_____

_____

Write about a situation in which you felt embarrassed to do something. What did you do? What do you think is the best way to avoid making things worse in this kind of situation?

_____

_____

_____

38

THE
WRONG THING
TO SAY
_____
_____
_____
_____
_____

THE
RIGHT THING
TO SAY
_____
_____
_____
_____
_____

39

Later, Kristen's mom knocked on her door. She looked like she was about to "lose it." "Clean up your room or you won't get dinner!" she threatened. Kristen knew her mom would never follow through on her threat. So she just ignored her, which made her mom even angrier.

On the opposite page, write something that Kristen should say to her mom to make things better. Then write the wrong thing that Kristen could say.

What do you think would happen if Kristen chose the wrong thing to say to her mom?

_____

_____

_____

What do you think would happen if Kristen chose the right thing to say?

_____

_____

_____

Write a rule or principle that could help Kristen avoid this problem in the future.

_____

_____

_____

Write about a situation in which someone wanted you to do something that you really didn't want to do. Did you do it? What do you think is the best way to avoid making things worse in this kind of situation?

_____

_____

_____

40

The next day at recess, Kristen found the coolest bracelet on the playground. It was wrapped in some colored paper. As she was trying it on, Liane saw her and said, "Hey, Kristen, that's my bracelet. Thanks for returning it." Kristen just looked at her and said, "What makes you so sure it's yours? I found it. Finders keepers."

On the opposite page, write something that Kristen should say to Liane. Then write the wrong thing that Kristen could say.

What do you think would happen if Kristen chose the wrong thing to say to Liane?

_____

_____

_____

What do you think would happen if Kristen chose the right thing to say to Liane?

_____

_____

_____

Write a rule or principle that could help Kristen do the right thing in the future.

_____

_____

_____

Write about a situation in which you found something that wasn't yours, but you really wanted to keep it. What did you do? What do you think is the best way to avoid making things worse in this kind of situation?

_____

_____

_____

THE
WRONG THING
TO SAY

_____
_____
_____
_____
_____

THE
RIGHT THING
TO SAY

_____
_____
_____
_____

43

After school, Sara came over to play. Kristen knew that she shouldn't try to reach the top shelf where the candlesticks were displayed. But she really wanted to show Sara how pretty they were. You can probably guess what happened—one of the candlesticks fell out of her hand and smashed on the floor.

On the opposite page, write something that Kristen should say to her mother to make things better. Then write the wrong thing that Kristen could say.

What do you think would happen if Kristen chose the wrong thing to say to her mother?

_____

_____

_____

What do you think would happen if Kristen chose the right thing to say?

_____

_____

_____

Write a rule or principle that could guide Kristen if she had a similar problem in the future.

_____

_____

_____

Write about a situation in which you did something and got into big trouble for it. What did you do? What do you think is the best way to avoid making things worse in this kind of situation?

_____

_____

_____

44

THE WRONG THING TO SAY

_____
_____
_____
_____
_____

THE RIGHT THING TO SAY

_____
_____
_____
_____
_____

45

That night, Petra called Kristen to ask her to go to the movies on Saturday, but Kristen said, "Why would I want to go with you?! You're the teacher's pet! Everyone would laugh at me if I went with you."

On the opposite page, write something that Kristen should say to Petra. Then write the wrong thing that Kristen could say.

What do you think would happen if Kristen was mean to Petra?

_____

_____

_____

What do you think would happen if Kristen was nice to Petra?

_____

_____

_____

Write a rule or principle that could help Kristen do the right thing in the future.

_____

_____

_____

Write about a situation in which someone you didn't like very much asked you to get together. What did you do? What do you think is the best way to avoid making things worse in this kind of situation?

_____

_____

_____

46

THE
WRONG THING
TO SAY

_____
_____
_____
_____
_____

THE
RIGHT THING
TO SAY

_____
_____
_____
_____
_____

47

Things at school weren't much better. During social studies, Kristen raised her hand so many times that she was about ready to give up. Why didn't the teacher call on her? She was so frustrated that she decided to raise both hands and wave them in the air. Now the teacher saw her—and told her to leave the room for five minutes for disrupting the class.

On the opposite page, write the right thing for Kristen to have done. Then write a wrong thing she could have done.

What do you think would happen if Kristen had done the right thing?

_____

_____

_____

What do you think would happen if Kristen had done the wrong thing?

_____

_____

_____

Write a rule or principle that could help Kristen remember to do the right thing in the future.

_____

_____

_____

Write about a situation in which you felt that someone was deliberately being mean to you. What did you do? What do you think is the best way to avoid making things worse in this kind of situation?

_____

_____

_____

48

THE
WRONG THING
TO SAY

_____
_____
_____
_____
_____

THE
RIGHT THING
TO SAY

_____
_____
_____
_____
_____

49

Kristen had always been a responsible kid. She was asked to take in the neighbors' newspaper and mail while they were on vacation. She forgot, and when the neighbors got home the mailbox was overflowing, and newspapers were strewn all over their yard. They were really angry. "What's the big deal?" Kristen thought. "Why are they so mad at me?

On the opposite page, write something that Kristen should say to the neighbors. Then write the wrong thing that Kristen could say.

What do you think would happen if Kristen said the right thing?

_____

_____

_____

What do you think would happen if Kristen said the wrong thing?

_____

_____

_____

Write a rule or principle that could help Kristen do the right thing in the future.

_____

_____

_____

Write about a situation in which you let people down and they were angry with you. What did you do? What do you think is the best way to avoid making things worse in this kind of situation?

_____

_____

_____

51

Kristen hated spending weekends with her dad. It was so boring! Plus, she worried about her mom being all alone. When he came to pick her up, she refused to go. But when she saw how disappointed he looked, she felt bad about hurting his feelings.

On the opposite page, write something that Kristen should say to her dad. Then write the wrong thing that Kristen could say.

What do you think would happen if Kristen said the right thing?

_____

_____

_____

What do you think would happen if Kristen said the wrong thing?

_____

_____

_____

Write a rule or principle that could help Kristen say the right thing in the future.

_____

_____

_____

Write about a situation in which you had to do something that you really didn't want to do. What did you do? What do you think is the best way to avoid making things worse in this kind of situation?

_____

_____

_____

THE
WRONG THING
TO SAY

THE
RIGHT THING
TO SAY

53

It seemed like things couldn't get worse. But when her dad said, "Kristen, you don't have to come with me now, even though I'd really like to spend some time with you. If it's okay with your mom, you can stay with her tonight and I'll pick you up tomorrow." Kristen thought, "I think I'd like that. Besides, we were going to the baseball game tomorrow anyway, and I don't want to miss that." She said, "Can we still go to the game, Dad?" "Sure, if you still want to," he answered. Kristen felt herself relaxing, and she decided that at the game there might be time to tell her dad about the things that were upsetting her.

On the opposite page, write something that Kristen could say to her dad that would help him understand how badly she was feeling and turn a negative situation into a positive one. Then write something that she could say that wouldn't help the situation at all.

What do you think would happen if Kristen helped to turn things around in a positive manner?

_____

_____

_____

What do you think would happen if Kristen decided not to do anything at all about the situation?

_____

_____

_____

Write a rule or principle that could help Kristen with a life change in the future.

_____

_____

_____

Write about a situation in which your life was changed and you felt like you couldn't do anything to stop it. What happened? What is the best way to avoid making things worse in this kind of situation?

_____

_____

_____

54

55

Marie had just moved to a new city, far away from her old home. She felt like nothing in her new life was the same, except her family, and they all seemed to be enjoying their new surroundings. "What's wrong with them?" she thought. "Don't they know everything here stinks?"

On Marie's first day at her new school, the girl across the aisle wouldn't stop staring at Marie. "I wish she would quit it," Marie thought to herself. "What's the matter with her? Why won't she quit staring at me? Why doesn't she just say something?"

On the opposite page, write something that Marie should say to the new girl to make things better. Then write the wrong thing that Marie could say to her.

What do you think would happen if Marie chose the wrong thing to say to the new girl?

_____

_____

_____

What do you think would happen if Marie chose the right thing to say to the new girl?

_____

_____

_____

Write a rule or principle that could help Marie avoid this problem in the future.

_____

_____

_____

Write about a situation in which someone made you uncomfortable. What did you do about it? What do you think is the best way to avoid making things worse in this kind of situation?

_____

_____

_____

56

57

It turned out that Laura (the girl in Marie's class) was staring at her because she wanted to be friendly. They made a play date and had a really good time. But then Marie's mom came to pick her up at Laura's house. "Come on, Marie," her mom said. "I have so much to do. We have to get home—now." Marie ignored her. "Let's go!" her mom shouted. "I hate her," Marie thought. "I wish I could live at Laura's house."

On the opposite page, write something that Marie should say to her mom. Then write the wrong thing that Marie could say to her.

What do you think would happen if Marie chose the wrong thing to say to her mom?

_____

_____

_____

What do you think would happen if Marie chose the right thing to say?

_____

_____

_____

Write a rule or principle that could help Marie avoid this problem in the future.

_____

_____

_____

Write about a situation in which someone made you do something you didn't want to do. What happened? What do you think is the best way to avoid making things worse in this kind of situation?

_____

_____

_____

Marie decided to try out for the baseball team with Laura. She didn't make it, but Laura did. Laura was so happy. She told Marie to come to watch the first game, but all Marie wanted to do was go somewhere so she could be alone and cry.

On the opposite page, write something that Marie should say to Laura. Then write the wrong thing that Marie could say to her.

What do you think would happen if Marie chose the wrong thing to say to Laura?

_____

_____

_____

What do you think would happen if Marie chose the right thing to say to Laura?

_____

_____

_____

Write a rule or principle that could help Marie avoid this problem in the future.

_____

_____

_____

Write about a situation in which you wanted something really badly but it didn't happen. What did you do? What do you think is the best way to avoid making things worse in this kind of situation?

_____

_____

_____

60

61

Marie's mom decided to be "helpful" and invited another girl, Katie, to spend the night. Katie came early that morning, but by the evening Marie was tired of her. After dinner, Marie went into her room and shut the door, leaving Katie in the living room by herself. "Marie," her mom said, "you can't leave Katie alone like this. She's your guest, and you have to make the best of it."

On the opposite page, write something that Marie should say to Katie. Then write the wrong thing that Marie could say to her.

What do you think would happen if Marie chose the wrong thing to say to Katie?

_____

_____

_____

What do you think would happen if Marie chose the right thing to say to Katie?

_____

_____

_____

Write a rule or principle that could help Marie avoid this problem in the future.

_____

_____

_____

Write about a situation in which you had to "make the best of" a situation. What happened? What do you think is the best way to avoid making things worse in this kind of situation?

_____

_____

_____

63

Marie was angry with her dad because he was always busy working at his new job. He'd come home from his job, eat dinner, and then work some more. She found his watch on the kitchen table and hid it in the cookie jar. When her dad asked her if she'd seen his watch, she told him she had no idea where it was. When he found it a few days later, he asked her why she'd hidden it.

On the opposite page, write something that Marie should say to her dad. Then write the wrong thing that Marie could say to him.

What do you think would happen if Marie chose the wrong thing to say to her dad?

_____

_____

_____

What do you think would happen if Marie chose the right thing to say to him?

_____

_____

_____

Write a rule or principle that could help Marie avoid this problem in the future.

_____

_____

_____

Write about a situation in which you did something to hurt someone. Why did you do it? What do you think is the best way to avoid making things worse in this kind of situation?

_____

_____

_____

Marie hated her new teacher. "Why can't Ms. Long be more like my old teacher?" she thought as she stared at the back of Harry's head in class. "What a dork," she thought. She got an idea. Wadding a little ball of paper, she put it in her mouth and then into the pen she'd emptied for spitballs. THWACK! The spitball hit dead center, and Harry whirled around. The teacher stopped and stared straight at her. "Uh oh," Marie thought. "Now I'm in for it."

On the opposite page, write something that Marie should say to the teacher. Then write the wrong thing that Marie could say to her.

What do you think would happen if Marie chose the wrong thing to say to the teacher?

_____

_____

_____

What do you think would happen if Marie chose the right thing to say to the teacher?

_____

_____

_____

Write a rule or principle that could help Marie avoid this problem in the future.

_____

_____

_____

Write about a situation in which you misbehaved at school. What happened? What do you think is the best way to avoid making things worse in this kind of situation?

_____

_____

_____

66

67

Marie's parents were so excited when they announced that the whole family was invited to a party. "I'm not going," Marie declared. "Yes, you are," said her mom, "and so is everyone else." "They can't make me go," Marie thought. "If they do, I'm gonna trash the place, and they'll really be sorry."

On the opposite page, write something that Marie should say to her mother. Then write the wrong thing that Marie could say to her.

What do you think would happen if Marie chose the wrong thing to say to her mother?

_____

_____

_____

What do you think would happen if Marie chose the right thing to say to her mother?

_____

_____

_____

Write a rule or principle that could help Marie avoid this problem in the future.

_____

_____

_____

Write about a situation in which you had to do something that you really didn't want to do. What happened? What do you think is the best way to avoid making things worse in this kind of situation?

_____

_____

_____

"Bobby will need a haircut before the party," Marie heard her mom say. That gave Marie an idea. She sat her little brother in a kitchen chair. Ten minutes later, Bobby's locks were all over the floor and he looked like a cross between Bert and Ernie. When her dad came home, it didn't take long to find out who had done this, and he went to find Marie.

On the opposite page, write something that Marie should say to her dad. Then write the wrong thing that Marie could say to him.

What do you think would happen if Marie chose the wrong thing to say to her father?

_____

_____

_____

What do you think would happen if Marie chose the right thing to say to her father?

_____

_____

_____

Write a rule or principle that could help Marie avoid this problem in the future.

_____

_____

_____

Write about a situation in which you did something that you knew would get you in trouble. Why did you do it? What do you think is the best way to avoid making things worse in this kind of situation?

_____

_____

_____

70

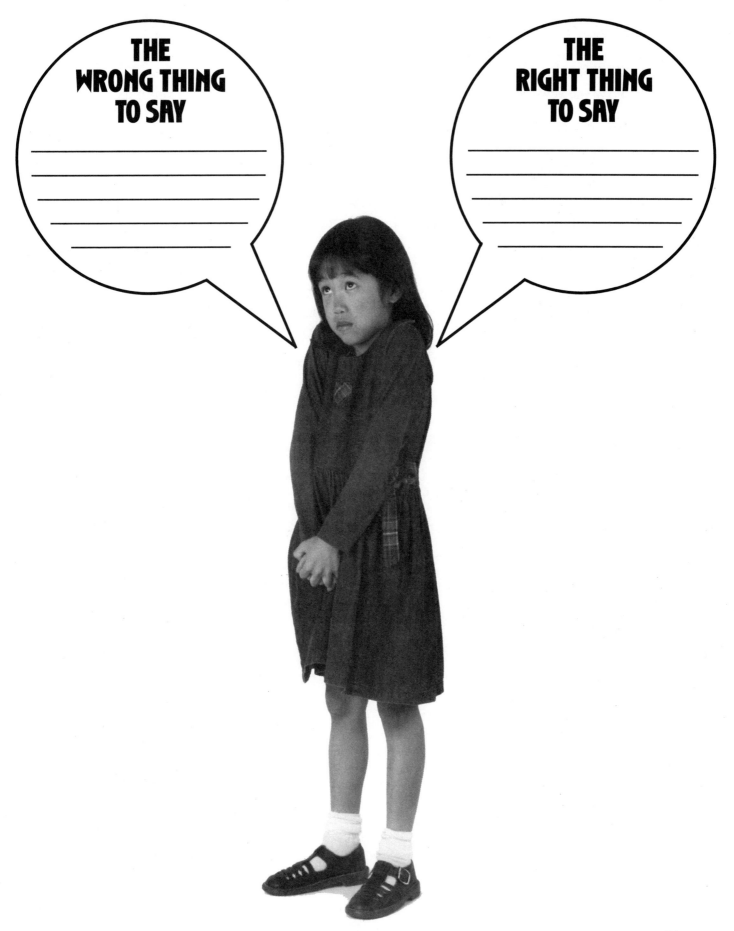

THE
WRONG THING
TO SAY
_____
_____
_____
_____
_____

THE
RIGHT THING
TO SAY
_____
_____
_____
_____

71

"Marie," her mom said, "can't you tell me what's wrong? I know you're having a hard time adjusting to the new school and neighborhood. Let's talk about it, and maybe you'll feel better."

On the opposite page, write something that Marie could say to her mom that would help her understand how badly she was feeling and turn a negative situation into a positive one. Then write something that she could say that wouldn't help the situation at all.

What do you think would happen if Marie tried to see the "good" in her situation?

_____

_____

_____

What do you think would happen if Marie decided not to do anything at all about the situation?

_____

_____

_____

Write a rule or principle that could help Marie with a life change in the future.

_____

_____

_____

Write about a situation in which your life was changed and you had to make the best of it. What happened? What is the best way to avoid making things worse in this kind of situation?

_____

_____

_____

72

Some people said that Darren was born angry. He never seemed to smile or have a kind word to say. When his teacher or his grandmother asked him, "How are you today?" he always made some sarcastic remark like, "How should I be? Life stinks." His parents didn't even bother to ask Darren how he was; they just assumed that he was unhappy. One day at dinner, Darren realized that his parents hadn't spoken to him all day. They said "do this" or "do that," but they hadn't really talked to him at all.

On the opposite page, write in something that Darren might say to his parents to start a real conversation. Write in something that he could say that would show that he cared about his parents' opinion, and then write something he might say that could make things even worse.

_____

_____

_____

What do you think would happen if Darren started a conversation with his parents and showed interest in them? Do you think that they would be responsive?

_____

_____

_____

What do you think would happen if Darren made some smart or angry remark in trying to get his parents' attention?

_____

_____

_____

Write a rule or principle that could help Darren relate better to adults.

_____

_____

_____

Write about a time when you or someone you know was unpleasant to be around. Did anything happen to make things better?

_____

_____

_____

THE WRONG THING TO SAY

THE RIGHT THING TO SAY

75

Darren's bad attitude particularly disturbed his teacher. Ms. Arnold once told Darren that she thought he was smart, but he just didn't seem to care about school or anything else. Unfortunately, that didn't seem to make much of an impression on Darren, because he had heard adults say things like this to him all his life. The fact was that he *didn't* really care about school or anything else!

Imagine that Darren had two voices that he could listen to: one that would keep him uninterested in school and the other that would "wake him up" and tell him to start caring about school before it was too late. On the opposite page, write in what each voice might say to him.

What do you think will happen to Darren if he doesn't change his attitude about school?

_____

_____

_____

What do you think will happen to Darren if he changes his attitude and starts applying himself? Is it too late?

_____

_____

_____

Write something that could motivate *you* to try harder, even though you didn't want to.

_____

_____

_____

Can you think of a time when an adult was disappointed or mad at you because you didn't seem to care? Did you do anything about it?

_____

_____

_____

76

Sometimes Darren felt badly that he couldn't seem to do anything right. Whatever people seemed to expect of him, he seemed to do the opposite. His father wanted him to be a good student, but he got poor grades. His mother wanted him to be "well-behaved," but he always did things that made her angry at him. He wanted to have a more positive attitude about things, but he didn't know how.

On the opposite page, write something that Darren could say to himself about his future that would be more positive. Then write something that would be negative.

Why do you think that some people seem to think negatively all of the time?

_____

_____

_____

What do you think makes other people always look at the positive side of a problem?

_____

_____

_____

Have you ever heard the expression "Smile and the world smiles with you. Frown and you frown alone?" What do you think it means?

_____

_____

_____

Write about a situation where you could be more positive in your thinking. Write exactly what you might say to yourself.

_____

_____

_____

78

Most of the time, Darren acted like he didn't need anybody at all. But then one day, he noticed that a girl in his class (her name was Mavis) seemed to be paying attention to him. Mavis said "hello" to him every day when he got on the school bus, and she would sometimes sit at his table in the cafeteria. Darren thought that he should do something to show Mavis that he liked her, but he had no idea what to do.

On the opposite page, write something that Darren might be thinking that would help him show Mavis that he was interested in her. Then write something that Darren might be thinking that would probably be the wrong thing to do or say.

_____

_____

_____

Write some advice that you might give Darren to start a conversation with Mavis or anyone else whom he wanted to get to know better.

_____

_____

_____

Write about a time when you felt that you wanted to get to know someone better, like a new friend. What did you do?

_____

_____

_____

80

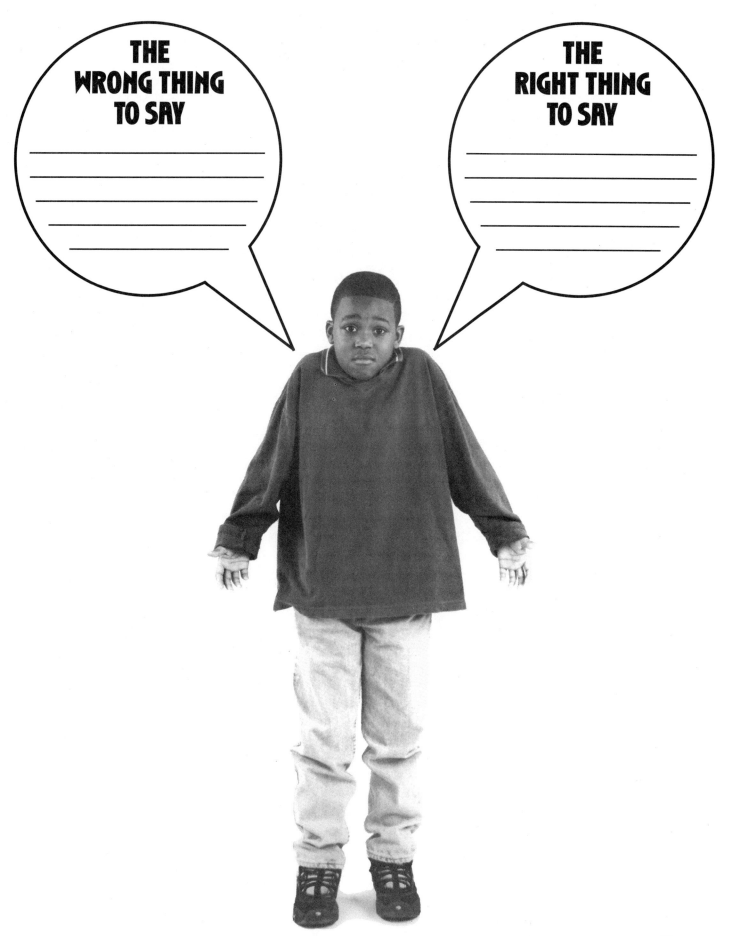

THE
WRONG THING
TO SAY

THE
RIGHT THING
TO SAY

81

Darren decided that he would try to impress Mavis. When he felt like making an effort, Darren was a good athlete, and he was particularly good at basketball. He thought that if he went out for the basketball team, Mavis might be interested in him. He had thought about going out for the team before, but he didn't like the coach because he thought he picked on him.

On the opposite page, write something that Darren could say to himself to keep up his enthusiasm. Then write something he might say that would be self-defeating.

What do you think would happen if Darren showed up for basketball practice with a different approach? What would he say to the coach that might change things?

_____

_____

_____

What do you think would happen if Darren showed up to practice with the same "chip on his shoulder?"

_____

_____

_____

How can you get people to change their attitude towards you?

_____

_____

_____

Can you think of something that you could do or say differently to make someone see you as a more cooperative person? Write it below.

_____

_____

_____

THE
WRONG THING
TO SAY

_____
_____
_____
_____
_____

THE
RIGHT THING
TO SAY

_____
_____
_____
_____
_____

83

Darren went to the team tryouts every day for a week. He tried as hard as he could to impress the coach. But at the end of the week, when the team was announced, Darren wasn't selected.

On the opposite page, write something that Darren could say to himself to help him deal with his disappointment. Then write something that Darren might say to himself that would only make him feel worse.

_____

_____

_____

How do you think Darren could deal with his disappointment in a positive way?

_____

_____

_____

What might happen if Darren gave in to his negative thinking?

_____

_____

_____

Some people think that learning to deal with disappointment and even failure is important. Why would they say this?

_____

_____

_____

Can you think of a time when you were very disappointed because you didn't get something you thought you deserved? How did you handle the situation? Looking back, do you think that was a good way to handle it?

_____

_____

_____

84

85

The next week, the coach of the basketball team stopped Darren in the hall and told him that he thought he had a lot of "promise," but he needed to keep practicing. On another day, his teacher told him that he seemed to be paying more attention in school, and she hoped that he would keep it up. Even his parents seemed to treat him better. His father asked him if he wanted to see a professional basketball game with him on the weekend, and his mother made his favorite dessert for dinner for no reason at all.

On the opposite page, write something that Darren might be thinking that would acknowledge this change in the way that people were treating him in a positive way. Then write something that Darren might be thinking that would be a negative interpretation of these events.

Write down a way that Darren could change to keep his parents and teachers treating him better.

_____

_____

_____

What do you think would happen if Darren didn't acknowledge these changes in the way people treated him?

_____

_____

_____

Why do you think that Darren's parents and teachers suddenly changed the way they were relating to him? Or was this really a change at all?

_____

_____

_____

Have you ever had a time when people seemed to be reacting to you differently? Did you do anything different yourself? Name some ways that people show they are trying to help you and they care about you.

_____

_____

_____

86

THE WRONG THING TO SAY

_____
_____
_____
_____
_____
_____

THE RIGHT THING TO SAY

_____
_____
_____
_____
_____
_____

87

Miguel was angry because his parents wouldn't buy him what he wanted. Miguel wanted new clothes, a new video game, and a new baseball glove, but his parents didn't seem to care.

On the opposite page, write something that Miguel might be thinking that would show that he felt sorry for himself. Then write something that Miguel could be thinking to show that he understood his parents' point of view.

How do you think Miguel's parents might react to his complaining that he never got what he wanted?

_____

_____

_____

How do you think Miguel's parents would treat him if they saw that he was more understanding of them?

_____

_____

_____

Empathy is a word that means you understand the feelings or point of view of others. Write below why this is important.

_____

_____

_____

Can you think of a time when you disagreed with your parents because you didn't understand their point of view? Write about what happened below.

_____

_____

_____

89

Most of all, Miguel wanted new sneakers. All his friends had Air Flight sneakers (some even had two pairs), but Miguel only had the cheap sneakers that his mother had bought at the discount store. Miguel would do anything to get Air Flight sneakers.

On the opposite page, write something that Miguel might say to himself about the sneakers that he wanted. Then write something that he might say to himself which would reflect the values of his parents.

What would happen if Miguel went through his life always being mad about something that he did not have?

_____

_____

_____

How do you think life might be different for Miguel if he was not so concerned about "material" things?

_____

_____

_____

Some people seem to be happy with very little, and other people never seem to be happy no matter what they have. Why do you think this is?

_____

_____

_____

Can you think of something that you really wanted but never got? Write down what happened.

_____

_____

_____

THE WRONG THING TO SAY

_____
_____
_____
_____
_____

THE RIGHT THING TO SAY

_____
_____
_____
_____
_____

91

Miguel's parents said that they didn't have enough money to spend on expensive sneakers. His father said, "Your mother and I work very hard for our money, and we can't waste it on things that are unimportant. Spending a hundred dollars on a pair of sneakers would be very foolish if you can get sneakers that are just as good for twenty dollars."

On the opposite page, write a negative thought that Miguel might be having after hearing his father's explanation. Now write down a positive thought that would help him accept what his father is telling him.

What do you think would happen if Miguel went through life always wishing for something that he didn't have?

_____

_____

_____

How do you think Miguel might learn to be more realistic?

_____

_____

_____

Do you know someone who is always dissatisfied with what he has? How do people treat him?

_____

_____

_____

Describe a situation where you wanted something that was really impossible for you to have. What did you do?

_____

_____

_____

THE
WRONG THING
TO SAY

_____
_____
_____
_____
_____

THE
RIGHT THING
TO SAY

_____
_____
_____
_____
_____

93

Miguel wished he had nicer parents. He thought about all the ways that his parents were unfair to him. They made him come right home from school, when he wanted to hang around the stores. They made him go to bed at 10 p.m., when everyone he knew went to bed at midnight. They made him do his homework before dinner or he couldn't watch TV at night.

On the opposite page, write something that Miguel might say to himself that would show that he thought his parents were unfair. Then write something that would show he understood his parents' point of view about the rules they thought were important.

What do you think might happen to Miguel if he continued to think that his parents' rules were unfair?

_____

_____

_____

How do you think Miguel's parents would treat him if he showed them that he respected their rules?

_____

_____

_____

Why is it important for children to follow the rules at home?

_____

_____

_____

Can you think of a rule in your home that you didn't agree with? Did you find a way to express your opinion without being disrespectful or disobedient?

_____

_____

_____

THE WRONG THING TO SAY

_____
_____
_____
_____
_____

THE RIGHT THING TO SAY

_____
_____
_____
_____
_____

95

Miguel knew some boys who were in a gang. They did what they wanted, and nobody gave them any trouble. They acted like they didn't even have any parents! They stayed out late, skipped school if they didn't feel like going, and if they wanted something from a store, they just took it. Miguel knew that they shoplifted things from stores (he even saw them do it), and they never seemed to get caught.

On the opposite page, write something Miguel might be saying to show that he was tempted to steal something. Then write something that his conscience would say to prevent him from stealing.

Do you know people who steal? What do you think of them?

_____

_____

_____

Can you think of a famous person who is known for his or her honesty? Why is it important to be honest, even about little things?

_____

_____

_____

What does having a "guilty conscience" mean?

_____

_____

_____

Have you ever done something that you felt guilty about? Have you ever stopped yourself from doing something that you knew was wrong?

_____

_____

_____

THE WRONG THING TO SAY

_____
_____
_____
_____
_____

THE RIGHT THING TO SAY

_____
_____
_____
_____
_____

97

One day after school, Miguel went up to Joey, who he knew was a member of the gang. Miguel said he wanted to join the gang and do the things that they did. Miguel said, "And I'll take stuff too. I'm not scared. Whatever you say to do, I'll do it."

On the opposite page, write what Miguel might be saying to himself to justify his joining Joey's gang. Then write what his conscience might be telling him.

What do you think happens to people who don't care about rules or laws?

_____

_____

_____

Do you know of anyone who didn't seem to care about rules but then changed?

_____

_____

_____

How can you judge a group of people to know whether you share the same values?

_____

_____

_____

Can you think of a group of kids your age that would be a *good* group for you to join? What do they do that you like or admire?

_____

_____

_____

98

THE
WRONG THING
TO SAY

_____
_____
_____
_____

THE
RIGHT THING
TO SAY

_____
_____
_____
_____

99

Joey said that Miguel should come to a gang meeting that afternoon and bring cigarettes and candy for everyone. He said, "You'll have to buy the cigarettes, because the guy keeps them under the counter; but while he's getting the cigarettes, you can stuff some candy in your jacket."

Miguel did just what he was told. He couldn't believe that the store owner sold him cigarettes so easily, or that he didn't even notice that he was taking candy. He went back to the gang, and they hung out and smoked and ate the candy that Miguel had brought. Some of the kids had brought beer, and Miguel tried some beer for the first time.

On the opposite page, write what Miguel might be thinking to justify his behavior to himself. Then write what his conscience might be telling him.

Suppose the store owner had caught Miguel. What do you think would have happened?

_____

_____

_____

Suppose that someone wanted to join a group, but refused to do certain things that she knew were wrong. What do you think would happen?

_____

_____

_____

Peer pressure sometimes makes people do things they know they shouldn't do. How can people resist peer pressure?

_____

_____

_____

Have you ever done something that you knew you shouldn't because of peer pressure? How did it turn out?

_____

_____

_____

THE
WRONG THING
TO SAY

THE
RIGHT THING
TO SAY

101

That night, Miguel felt sick to his stomach. He had smoked cigarettes, drank beer, and ate three bars of candy. His parents thought that Miguel had a virus and told him to go to bed and see if he felt better in the morning.

On the opposite page, write what Miguel might be saying to himself to feel better. Then write what his conscience might be saying.

Do you think that most people in jail started out like Miguel as young kids?

_____

_____

_____

Do you think that people can stop themselves from doing things that they know are wrong? How does this happen?

_____

_____

_____

What do you think is the difference between people who learn from their mistakes and those who don't?

_____

_____

_____

Some people say that in the end "everyone gets what they deserve." What do you think this means?

_____

_____

_____

103

The next morning was Saturday, and Miguel slept until 9 am. He felt better and was glad to see that his father wasn't angry when he came to the breakfast table. Miguel not only felt sick to his stomach; he also felt guilty for stealing, for lying to his parents, and for drinking and smoking.

Then Miguel got the shock of his life!

"I know all about you and that gang of boys," his father said calmly. "I know what happened, and I think I know why it happened. We're going to talk all about it tonight. But for now, I want you to go to the store where you stole the candy, right after breakfast, and start your job. You're going to work there every Saturday and first pay back the money for the candy that you stole, and then you can start earning money to buy those sneakers that you want."

On the opposite page, write Miguel's first reaction to what his father told him. Then write a statement that shows that Miguel understands what his father has done.

Do you think Miguel has learned his lesson?

_____

_____

_____

What do you think will happen the next time Miguel sees Joey?

_____

_____

_____

Have you ever heard the expression, "Let the punishment fit the crime?" How do you think this applies to Miguel's situation?

_____

_____

_____

Miguel's father found a positive way to handle his son's problem. Can you think of a time when you found a positive solution to handle one of your own problems?

_____

_____

_____

104

105